Shades Of Khaki & other poems

WILLIAM CLARKE

HARRY CHAMBERS/PETERLOO POETS

First published in 1976
by Harry Chambers/Peterloo Poets
8 Cavendish Road, Heaton Mersey
Stockport SK4 3DN, Cheshire

ISBN 0 905291 02 6

Printed in Great Britain by
The Scolar Press Limited, Ilkley, Yorkshire

SHADES OF KHAKI
AND OTHER POEMS

William Clarke

ACKNOWLEDGEMENTS are due to the editors of *John Bull*, *The Countryman*, *The Lady*, *Phoenix*, *The Poetry Review*, *Punch* and *The Pick of Punch*, *Reveille*, *Scottish Secondary Teachers' Association Magazine*, *The Times Literary Supplement*, *Tribune*, *Truth* and '*X*' *Review*, in whose pages some of these poems first appeared.

For Elsa — my wife

CONTENTS

SHADES OF KHAKI

OTHER POEMS

SHADES OF KHAKI

War Poets

We are prepared to give them credit for
The promise that remained all unfulfilled
Being assured they volunteered for war,
That they were very young and they were killed.
It is the coming back we can't forgive;
The smug presumption of a will to live.

Military Cemetery

Such discipline on parade
Would put to shame a Guards' Brigade;
So long, so rigid, to remain like this
And still no order to dismiss.

Bayonet Practice

Every Friday, two to four,
Because the Colonel can't forget,
We line up facing sacks of straw,
Our backs to the atomic war,
And practise with the bayonet.

Church Parade

Herded like silly sheep
In our allotted pews
We listen, half asleep,
While Parson airs his views.

In high official flight
We take off from our knees
And bleat about the right
To worship as we please.

Checked on the Big Parade
(Some item out of place)
Nothing that Parson said
Can lessen our disgrace.

And heaven has, I fear,
No dispensating cup
For we are only here
To make the numbers up.

The General

He jams the traffic and, for miles around,
        Astride his granite horse all progress bars;
And I recall the way he stood his ground
        When tanks took over from his gay hussars.

Looters

It seems they'd left the shop in such a hurry
The stock was still arranged upon the shelves,
So when the fellows got down from the lorry
The sergeant simply said to help ourselves

To cigarettes and matches, which we did,
Except that one guy with a conscience still
Took from his tattered wallet half a quid
And rang the change up on the battered till.

We bore with him, of course. We even joked
About his scruples being sadly wasted;
But it was quite some time before we smoked
And then how bitter the tobacco tasted.

African Soldiers

Surprised to see his order
Smartly carried out
The N.C.O., still conscious
Of uniform and rank,
Began to realise
What Empires were about
And how the white man's gold
Got in the white man's bank.
All one needed was
The temerity to shout,
Backed up, as it were,
By aeroplane and tank.

Mediterranean

Gibraltar, when you wake and come on deck,
Looms up so vast and blots out Europe so
You feel you've wandered down a cul-de-sac
And, but for turning, there's no place to go.

It's different at Valetta; there the eye
Takes in the pattern of the land by stages,
Like opening a jewelled fan against the sky
Or turning over illuminated pages.

Somewhere, far off, a cigarette burns grey;
The coast of Africa, they say.

Troop-Ship

One day they sent me up
To scrub the officers' Mess;
I never knew how big
The Nevassa was till then.

A Tank

A small patch only of a stretch
Of grass remains; two blocks of council flats
Share it between them. All along this road
Were similar patches once, occasional shops,
The eye-sore, even then, of poster boards.

And here, the tank. One of the veterans
Used at Cambrai, I think. I must have been
No more than seven and was lifted up
To put some coppers in the collecting box,
For wounded soldiers?

Where the road now runs
Streaming with cars I cross, eventually,
And try to decipher in the new-mown lawn
Trace of the standing weight of its occupation:
What foolish fancies old men have.

The Barracks

Once I wept, being a new recruit
In the old barracks on the edge of town,
Because I could not learn to drill and shoot;
But now I weep to see it half pulled down.

I would much rather they had cleared the space
Or finished building the new office block
Or Supermarket that will take its place;
It might have proved a salutary shock.

But I would have been spared this walking round
Looking at doors and windows gaping wide
And letting fancy shape for me the sound
Of all the life that dwindled here and died.

I would have quickly passed and quite forgot
Nor ever resurrected for re-trial
The old regret that roots me to this spot:
Half-truths are worse than a bare-faced denial.

War Memorial (1)

One poppy-wreath, I noticed, lasted well
Into the Spring before it began to wear
As shabby as all the rest and in its turn
Was carted off to the corporation dump.

Sometime in June somebody put a bunch
Of roses where they first were trodden on
Then washed away in the rain, not being rooted
Where they might have bloomed.

The nominal roll
From Pte. Adams to Sgt. Zebeddee
Now looks as blank and irrelevant to the times
As the gilt-listed Mayors in the Town Hall,
Stripped of their honours and their robes and chains.

War Memorial (2)

One name's been added to the heroic score,
Scratched with a penknife on the granite base;
'Kilroy' was here who never went to War
And felt the need to justify his case.

Return To Base

The place had not changed to the extent
That here and there you couldn't recognise
Signs of its occupation during the war,
The backstreet billets and the pubs you spent
Off-duty hours in after an exercise,
The Sergeant's Mess over the Co-op store
And the old mansion in its yew-tree shade
That served as headquarters of the brigade.

It all looked pretty much the same and yet
Was not the same because the people there
Seemed unapproachable or chose to ignore
What brought you back that made you stand and stare,
The young too young to remember or forget;
The old too old to care much anymore.

OTHER POEMS

Pied Piper

A simple tune is more
Than symphonies. It comes
Unbidden through the door
Into the heart, and drums
And loud sounding brass
And violins en masse
Don't get so easily through
As penny whistles do.

The Keepsake

My father smoked the same old pipe for years
Till all the family were reduced to tears,
But being master in his own domain,
We coughed, but lacked the courage to complain.

Yet, opening Mother's writing desk today,
I found the charred old relic tucked away
With half a dozen other things she prized
More than we children ever realized.

And I was moved as much as now I know
She must have been, those lonely years ago,
Seeing the ash at bottom of the bowl
And never a flame to give it life and soul.

After The Funeral (1)

Father used to complain he couldn't rest
On Sunday afternoon because of the row
The children made.
                    If he could come back now,
Stealing upstairs, while in our Sunday best
We sit bewildered in the drawing room,
He would appreciate the perfect peace
Of drawn curtains, lavender and lace,
After the chatter of birds about his tomb.

Isolationist

My father was a lonely man;
None of us bothered much about him
Until our pleasures we out-ran
And felt we could not do without him,
When to our deep concern we found
It bored him having us around.

Old People's Home

I asked him could his children not
Provide a home for him instead
Of leaving him up here to rot?
It didn't worry him, he said.

He used to wish them miles away
When they were kids and made a row;
It was to be expected they
Should turn the tables on him now.

Father And Child

The day I knew
We both were growing old
Was when she took my arm
Instead of my hand,
First shyly, then
With each step growing bold
As if she wanted me to understand
She was no longer to be led
And I
Would do to lean on
Till she learned to fly.

Age Of Innocence

Old men have little patience
With children when they've seen
Their own grow up unkindly,
However kind they've been.

So when a ball comes over
The wall or tiny shoes
Trample the prize geraniums
They are not slow to abuse

The luckless small offender,
Not for what he has done
But for having a foolish father,
Proud of his foolish son.

Lovers' Meeting

Seeing her yesterday I thought with a start
How old she looked who was so young in heart
And I was glad she passed me by unknowing
Till I reflected it was her way of showing
The years had wrought the same sad change in me
And robbed us both of our identity.

Children's Concert

It wasn't that Elaine went flat
    And Jenny piped her eye;
As parents we allowed for that;
    A child can only try.

What irritated most was this:
    Matilda stopped the show
By using every artifice
    A nice girl shouldn't know.

Dolls

Dolls are immortal children
Never fated to lose
Their innocence or grow
Out of their tiny shoes.

They are never as lonely
As we are. There remains
Always another child
To breathe life in their veins.

Or we surprise in them
Opening a cupboard door,
The dead child in ourselves
We thought to see no more.

Hands

Hands have no life of their own till they take hold
Of something tangible, or simply fold
On other hands, in prayer, or making friends:
Else there is nothing quite so dead as hands.

You watch an old man nodding in his chair,
His bony fingers clutching at empty air,
And then consider if hands we do not use
Are not as pathetic as cast-off shoes:

Or marionettes, no longer jerked on strings:
Or silent roundabouts, or empty swings.

Tower And Spire

Towers are impressive, but the climbing eye
Gets hooked up on the detail overhead,
Whereas a steeple simply pricks the sky
And draws you with it like a piece of thread.

Elegy

Whether or not you raise
The money to raise a stone
After a lapse of days
The dead are left alone.

And better then no name
Over the mound of earth
Than one that seems to shame
Grief for what it is worth.

Here is Anne, aged three,
Covered with rank grass
And mourned only by me
Who never knew the lass.

After The Funeral (2)

She would have been surprised could she have seen
The corsage he bought to celebrate
The end of the affair. A little late
To come bearing gifts he might have been
But never let it be said that he was mean
With the insurance money at any rate.

In A Glasgow Primary School

Perched on the several rungs of a gilded cage
They were like birds, like budgerigars, she thought,
Mechanically intoning what she taught
Without the comprehension that comes with age.
They were to be inducted at every stage
With the bright baubles the authorities bought,
The beads, the plasticine, the cardboard fort,
The illustrations on the printed page,
Till such time as their natural inclination
To leap and dance and play at catch and can
Beyond the barriers of circumstance
Was harnessed to a self-determination
Befitting more the dignity of man
Who may not linger where he must advance.

School Caretaker

You can see from the grim satisfaction
He gets from wiping ciphers from the board
And feeding waste to the boiler fire
That he has come to terms with an old desire.
He still thinks education is a fraud
That must give way to the man of action
Armed with a broomstick for a sword.

Sea Pictures

Deep down and fathoms deep
    Are cities under the sea,
And there the sailors sleep
    Through all eternity.

They have no watch to do
    These idle mariners
Nor any need is theirs
    For captain or for crew.

Their harbours sub-marine
    Are silted up with sand
And no horizon line
    Tempts them from the land.

In windows where the blinds were down
    The red geraniums appear,
A stranger walking in the town
    Would never know that Grief was here.

The suits of customary black
    Have been discarded for the gay,
And if we talk about the Wreck
    It is in a familiar way.

Our mourning was like curtain-fall,
    A time to re-arrange the face,
To move one picture from the wall
    And put another in its place.

Oldest Inhabitant

He knows what lies concealed where highways hurry
And won't be stopped from telling any man,
Whose interest is only momentary
Or needs reviving with a watering-can,
What flowering fields there were where
        children cherished
The never end to their recurring Spring
And how much would inevitably have perished
But for his habit of remembering.

Gulls

They let the wind decide
Their course of action.
So do I . . .
With far less satisfaction.